Pandemic Blessings:

STORIES OF THANKSGIVING IN AN UNUSUAL TIME

Presented by: Jennifer Formoso

Enhanced DNA Publishing
DenolaBurton@EnhancedDNA1.com
317-537-1438

Pandemic Blessings
Stories of Thanksgiving in an Unusual Time
Copyright © 2021 Jennifer Formoso

Contributors:
Julia Hrysenko, Sally Hribar, Harriet Ayers, Noemi Falcone, Sonya Ruff Jarvis, Lilly Rios, Evelys M. Rios-Lopez, Roxanne C. August, Renee Sheckfee, Jonette Lucio, Amber Peckham, Juszina Maria, Ching Chuang-Chow, Norma I. Castro, Gwendolyn Blake, Stacey Tuhey, Rosa Almazan, Melahni Ake

Cover Artist: Nicole Powell – www.NPInspired.com

ISBN-13: 978-1-7369079-8-6
Library of Congress Number: 2021922061

DEDICATION

G iving thanks to God first and foremost, I'd like to dedicate this book to all the front line, essential workers who have tirelessly and selflessly given us so much of themselves during this pandemic. We hold space in our hearts for you, and are so grateful!

To all those who have lost loved ones to the COVID-19 pandemic, I dedicate this book to you as well. We pray for you to find strength, hope, and a measure of God's peace that passes all understanding in your healing journey.

Last, but not least, I dedicate this book to family. Thank you to my dad for teaching me humility and gentleness, and to my mom for teaching me determination and perseverance in the face of adversity. To my younger brother Kenny, who annoyed me earlier in life, but who has become my close, trusted sibling and friend, please know how grateful I am that you helped pave the way for me to be baptized as a Christian in my adult life.

To my wonderful husband, Juan, thank you for your patience with me during the process of my becoming a first-time author; and to our beautiful daughter who made us parents, thank you Serena. We love you and are so proud of you.

Deepest gratitude as well to my wonderful publisher, Denola Burton, and to the eighteen amazing and Godly women whose personal and moving stories made this book possible.

There are so many more of you I want to thank. You know who you are, and I love and appreciate you all.

"Do not be anxious about anything, but in every situation, by prayer and petition, with thanksgiving, present your requests to God. And the peace of God, which transcends all understanding, will guard your hearts and your minds in Christ Jesus." (Philippians 4: 6-7)

TABLE OF CONTENTS

DEDICATION..i

INTRODUCTION.. v

JENNIFER'S STORY.. 1

JULIA'S STORY... 11

NOEMI'S STORY 15

HARRIET'S STORY... 21

SALLY'S STORY 25

SONYA'S STORY 29

RENEE'S STORY 37

LILLY'S STORY 43

EVELYS'S STORY... 49

ROXANNE'S STORY... 55

JONETTE'S STORY... 59

STACEY'S STORY... 65

AMBER'S STORY... 71

NORMA'S STORY.. 77

CHING'S STORY.. 81

JUSZINA'S STORY 85

GWEN'S STORY.. 91

MELAHNI'S STORY 97

ROSA'S STORY.. 105

CONCLUSION 107

Pandemic Blessings: Stories of Thanksgiving in an Unusual Time

INTRODUCTION

Back in January 2021, I asked a number of friends, family, church members, and co-workers if they could answer just three questions for me: How did you come to know Christ? What role has He played in your life to date? And what blessings, big or small, have you found amidst the COVID-19 pandemic despite the inherent challenges and struggles? I hesitated to put this out there, as so many people have lost so much as a result of this tragedy. People have lost loved ones, been separated from family and friends, had trouble making ends meet, and faced increasing relationship stressors amid worsening mental health issues. The list feels endless and there continue to be so many losses. But our God is Sovereign, our Lord is good, and He is always near to us. Isaiah 55:6-7 says, "Seek the LORD while he may be found; call on him while he is near." He is indeed near to the broken hearted and the weak. This pandemic has left us weakened but not defeated because we have Jesus as our comforter, refuge, strength, and as our Salvation. That is what made me put out the call to family, friends, church members, and anyone who knows Christ or wants to know Him.

The purpose of this book is to lift up the Lord even in the midst of what is undoubtedly one of the most challenging periods of our collective lifetimes and proclaiming His goodness and the blessings He has bestowed upon us throughout this season of hardship and loss. Here you will find not only my story as a Christ follower, but also the amazing and inspiring stories of fellow believers. These are stories of how they came to know and follow Christ, and what He has blessed them with during this difficult season. My hope is that their diverse stories and perspectives bless you as well in some way, in accordance with His will. We are the Body of Christ. *"Now you are the body of Christ, and each one of you is a part of it."* (1 Corinthians 12:27)

Jesus, take the pen….

I remember reading about David and Goliath and thinking…. how is that possible? The skeptic in me could not conceive of this playing out in real life. I felt the same way when I read the Scripture from Matthew, *"For truly I tell you, if you have faith the size of a mustard seed, you can say to this mountain, 'Move from here to there,' and it will move. Nothing will be impossible for you."* (Matthew 17:20.) I was ashamed of my doubt, rebellion, and disbelief. Years later, I am somewhat better able to understand the bigger picture and the true meaning in these verses. So, I ask you… what is your Goliath? What is your mountain that you want moved? The COVID-19 pandemic has certainly been just that for so many of us, individually as well as collectively. Who would ever have imagined back in March 2020 the enormous changes that loomed ahead of us all and that would significantly impact us on every conceivable life level? The pandemic changed life in untold ways and made so many of us slow down to reflect and really think about what is most important in life. I know that it did for me and my family, as we struggled to find our "new normal" and seek and find blessings even in the small things, despite the challenges and sadness. This was the silver lining, and here you will find other Christ followers who also sought and found blessings, both big and small, amongst the challenges and struggles inherent in living through this unprecedented experience.

JENNIFER'S STORY

For me, the pandemic brought fear and panic despite feeling rooted in my Christianity and the knowledge that God was and always is in control. How could I be so afraid when I had the Holy Spirit? January and February of 2020 brought sadness and worry, as well as prayers for those affected in parts of the world far away from my own world in Connecticut. I watched along with many others as an epidemic became a pandemic, as schools closed, as restaurants and businesses shut down, and as the world went remote in so many senses of the word. From remote work and school for my daughter and her classmates to remote conversations with friends and family, and an increasing sense of separation set in as we were further removed from close connections and relationships. I had panic attacks in my car before going into my local supermarket, something that was very unlike me during normal times. It felt like the world was getting smaller every day, and the little things I normally took for granted became more precious and important to me and my family.

My daughter, then a senior in high school, looked forward to our daily drives to Starbucks where we went through the drive thru with our masks on and an arsenal of Clorox wipes and hand sanitizer at our disposal. One day in April 2020 she said to me, "I look forward to these trips every day. It's like I never realized how important this was." A FaceTime call to a family member or friend, perhaps put off or avoided previously, became more meaningful. A chance to see a friend outdoors, even from a distance, was huge. Indeed, the things taken for granted pre-pandemic became special. These small blessings became big blessings this past year.

Christ was not present in my earlier years, at least not that I was aware of. I actually came to know Christ in my basement about 15 years ago. My mother-in-law gave me a box of old books to clean out her attic and I don't think she knew what was in there. I put it in my basement and her clutter became mine until the night that our basement was flooding. My husband Juan and I took turns staying awake overnight to monitor the situation, and at 2:00 a.m. I decided to check out the books to pass the time downstairs. One of the books towards the bottom was an old copy of The New Testament. I had never even seen it before, so I began to read…. and could not stop. It was like finding the missing piece of the puzzle on my faith journey.

I had grown up Jewish and lived a double life. My Dad was a non-practicing Protestant, my mom was Jewish, and they decided to raise me and my younger brother in the Jewish faith. Not completely, however. By day we attended a Yeshiva, learning Hebrew and studying the Old Testament, adhering strictly to Jewish laws and codes. On Saturdays, my father drove me to Synagogue to be with my school friends, and I ducked down as far as I could so as not to be seen by my friends who walked to Synagogue like good Jews, like real Jews, did. I was dropped off several blocks away in our New York City neighborhood, and walked the rest of the short way, once again blending in. I did this again and again for most of my childhood and teenage years. Looking into our rent-controlled apartment near Washington Heights in the 1970s and 1980s, one would not have known we were Jewish, or really anything discernible in terms of faith, spirituality, or religion.

My respect for the Jewish people and the Jewish faith is strong, especially because I would not necessarily have found Christ without having had that foundation of faith in God instilled by my teachers all those years ago. I'm sure that was not the intent or plan for a Yeshiva girl to struggle in her journey of faith up to the age of 39 when she discovered The New Testament in a box in the basement. Reading Isaiah and Matthew that night was like hearing an audible click, a proverbial lightbulb going off. God was telling me that I had finally found the missing piece of the puzzle. It finally made sense. I could see how everything lined up, how the pieces fit, and gained the knowledge that I have a real Savior who cared enough about me to die on the cross for my sins. I had never felt worthy, never thought I was enough, and that night was the beginning of my learning otherwise.

To be perfectly honest, I went back to my normal life the next day. I went to work, took care of my daughter, spent time with my husband, went to sleep, and did it all over again

3

the next day. I wasn't sure what I needed or even wanted to do with the new knowledge I had acquired in the middle of that October night. God had other plans for me.

I'm a social worker, in a school by day and in my office seeing clients on evenings and weekends. I had been struggling with the idea of attending a church, a big step for me which I was avoiding. When my daughter was 4 years old, I was unexpectedly informed by two of my regular Sunday morning clients, within two weeks of each other, that they could no longer come on Sundays due to a change in availability and needed to be seen on alternate days. I heard God saying to me "Now what?" I stepped into Crossroads Community Church in my town of Trumbull, CT on Sunday, April 20, 2008 with my daughter. My heart was beating so fast. This fake Jewish girl with her insecure inner child saying you're not enough, you won't fit in, and you're about to be struck down by God for even entering a church and looking at a cross. There were tables set up and Pastor Rich began leading a Passover Seder. I felt like Alice must have felt in Wonderland, falling down the rabbit hole. I was very confused. That day I learned that Jesus was a Jew, he ate at Passover Seders, and that the Last Supper was actually a Seder. I learned that I was welcome, I was loved, and the story of the New Testament was real and redeeming, life-giving and life-saving.

A lot has happened in my faith and my life in general since that day. I continued going to the same church and gave my life to Christ in a beautiful lakeside Baptism one year later, in September 2009. Three years later, my mom, Harriet, did the same at her church in Florida. My brother Kenny was baptized back in 2005. We consider ourselves blessed to have found Christ, or rather, for Him to have sought and not forsaken us.

I am a therapist, and my joy comes through helping others. I believe that it is my spiritual gift, and that we all have them. Paul tells us in his letter to the Corinthians, "There are different kinds of gifts, but the same Spirit distributes them. There are different kinds of service, but the same Lord. There are different kinds of working, but in all of them and in everyone it is the same God at work. Now to each one the manifestation of the Spirit is given for the common good." (1 Corinthians 12:4-7.) As someone who grew up with low self- esteem, it was nothing short of a miracle to find my worth in Christ and His teachings. I had a spiritual gift and I was part of something much bigger than my own life. I was a cherished part of the Body of Christ.

"Just as a body, though one, has many parts, but all its many parts form one body, so it is with Christ. For we were all baptized by[c] one Spirit so as to form one body—whether Jews or Gentiles, slave or free— and we were all given the one Spirit to drink. Even so the body is not made up of one part but of many." (1 Corinthians 12:12)

"Now you are the body of Christ, and each one of you is a part of it." (1 Corinthians 12:27)

This is what has gotten me through each day, and especially

during the pandemic. Each day I try to ask God to direct my steps, to help me see the bigger picture and help others as He would want. It became even more important to do so during the past year when the world dwindled down to the basics. Each minor outing, each connection, each small and seemingly insignificant part of the endless days became more and more significant, more and more of a blessing when looked at through a different lens.

I cried when I read people's stories here that were so generously shared and freely given to lift up the Lord and perhaps make a difference in others' lives. We are the Body of Christ. You, the one reading this, are a part of that same body and are loved by Jesus, whether you walk with Christ or are interested in walking with Him but unsure of what that means. The contributors to this anthology, myself included, are all Christ believers and followers, though we all fail and fall short of the Glory of God.

The pandemic, for me, brought life into sharper focus and helped me reevaluate what being blessed really means. Typically, blessings come in the form of a new marriage, a baby, a new job or a new home. Blessings come in the form of loving friendships and relationships, and sometimes blessings come in the form of physical healing or financial repair. But blessings also come in smaller ways, less obvious ways, especially during a pandemic that may have felt like a curse to many, not a blessing. This era in our lives has been unprecedented. As we have now learned, blessings may look very different during a pandemic.

When life dwindled down to next to nothing, I'll be honest, depression and anxiety set in for me. These were more frequent companions of mine years prior, but they came back in full force in March 2020, when this alien pandemic came to our doorsteps. I was reminded of Old Testament scenes of plagues, disease, and terror. The school where I work shut down, and we all thought it would be several weeks at the most to "flatten the curve." We watched in horror at what was happening in China, Italy, Spain, and then around the world as epidemic became pandemic. The unthinkable became reality for us here in the United States, too. There was little we could do and little control to be had.

We all like our control, don't we? It gives us a sense of security in a world where we often feel it is lacking, and we had even less so when life was quickly shutting down. But there were signs of hope and unity, even in the small things. The people singing on their balconies in Italy was one of the most beautiful and hopeful displays of the Body of Christ that I have ever witnessed. Jesus could be found everywhere, from balconies to visits outside windows, to grocery stores where people helped each other find scarce commodities and smiled at each other in unity even through their masks. He can be found in the big things and in the smallest details perhaps we never noticed or appreciated before. He could also be found in the losses, the many, many losses tragically brought about by this pandemic. The loss of life and loved ones including young people, who were not exempt. Funerals that could not be held, families that sadly, and shockingly, could not say their goodbyes. I am reminded of this passage from the Bible when Jesus Himself wept at the death of Lazarus, *"On his arrival, Jesus found that Lazarus had already been in the tomb for four days.... When Martha heard that Jesus was coming, she went out to meet him, but Mary stayed at home. "Lord," Martha said to Jesus, "if you had been here, my brother would not have died. When Jesus saw her weeping, and the Jews who had come along with her also weeping, he was deeply moved in spirit and troubled.... Jesus wept."* (John 11:35)

Jesus wept, and I believe he also wept for us during this pandemic. Although we don't fully understand why this happened, what we do know is that His ways and His thoughts are higher than ours. *"For my thoughts are not your thoughts, neither are your ways my ways, saith the LORD. For as the heavens are higher than the earth, so are my ways higher than your ways, and my thoughts than your thoughts."* (Isaiah 55:8-9)

If you have lost loved ones, you have my prayers and my heartfelt sympathy. There is nothing that can take away the pain and suffering you are enduring, but please know that others care for you. I pray that God fills your life with good, supportive people who lift you up and are there to encourage you each step of this difficult path. Seek them out. Continue to pray and talk with Jesus daily. *"God is our refuge and strength, a very present help in trouble. Therefore will not we fear, though the earth be removed, and though the mountains be carried into the midst of the sea; Though the waters thereof roar and be troubled, though the mountains shake with the swelling thereof. Selah."* (Psalm 46)

He is with you. He is with us all.

This pandemic, unprecedented in our lifetimes, has truly been a collective trauma. We have indeed gone through this together, as a community, as a nation, as a world. Although there has been divisiveness, I believe that the common struggles faced have helped us rise above the disunity more than we may realize. Most importantly, the blessings encountered amidst the challenges and suffering are the glue that hold us together and create in us not only a sense of survivorship, but of personal and community growth and development.

As you continue to read, you will encounter eighteen very personal and unique stories and perspectives written by various Christian contributors. These stories are intended to answer the original questions of how each believer came to know Christ, what role He has played in each of their lives, and how the COVID-19 pandemic has impacted them. Most central to the spirit in which this book is written, they will speak to blessings, both big and small, received during this challenging and difficult period in our collective lives. I hope their stories touch you as deeply as they have touched and blessed me.

I am *Jennifer Formoso*, a Christ-follower, mom, wife, daughter, social worker, beach-lover, and finally an author. I live in Trumbull, Connecticut with my husband Juan, and daughter, Serena. I work as both a school social worker as well as a psychotherapist. I consider helping others to be my spiritual gift, and it is my greatest honor and blessing aside from my role as a mother.

My favorite Bible verse is Jeremiah 29:11: *"For I know the plans I have for you," declares the Lord, "plans to prosper you and not to harm you, plans to give you hope and a future."*

JULIA'S STORY

My first memories of Christ are inextricably linked to my Catholic upbringing in New York City. We attended Mass every Sunday, and I went to Catholic school. I perceived there was the Church, and then there was Christ. However, I remember attending Good Friday services and feeling bereft. And then rejoicing on Easter. I recall the gravity of Holy Communion, and the solemnity of Confirmation. Christ was there, but among a thicket of rules and structures.

When I went to college, I fell away from church and Christ. This continued well into my 20's and 30's. There were some very dark times where I often found myself in a church, not praying, sometimes not even thinking, but needing to be close to Him. I sought him, instinctively, at my lowest times. I couldn't conceive that Jesus was always with me through good times or bad.

Later as a wife and mother, I rekindled that little flame of faith. I tried to raise my son as I had been raised. We attended Mass together, prayed at night, and stopped into church to "say hi to God." When my husband and I separated, I found myself wordless and broken in Church again. The next few years were hell, as my husband and I

11

divorced, and my parents passed away, all within a couple of years. I was angry at God. I no longer went to Church, and I stopped praying with my son. I ceased giving him any religious instruction. I lashed out.

This spiritual isolation continued for some time until my now adolescent son was in crisis. I started attending a Twelve Step program, as I needed a Higher Power. I couldn't do this on my own anymore. I finally realized that Christ had been beside me for all the good and bad moments, and would be, always. I needed His love, forgiveness, and strength, for myself and my son. I dedicated my son to Him in prayer, knowing that His plan is best. I have started going back to Church, but I also strive to pray and talk to Him every day. I am a work in progress, and I strive to know Christ daily.

I remained in NYC during the pandemic. We didn't have a choice. We had nowhere else we could go. I honestly have blotted out a lot of memories of that time. I remember the endless bleat of ambulance sirens in my neighborhood in March and April of 2020. Walking along the banks of the Hudson was my solace, and I felt grateful for every leaf and bud, every blossom that grew that spring. I would look at the Hudson, which changed colors every day, from jade green to gray, to cadet blue, to cream, every day different. Because the city was so quiet, I could hear the birds in the park much more clearly. I felt gratitude for the guys on the corner selling fruits and vegetables, when you couldn't go into the supermarket because the lines were so long outside. Making a racket at 7:00 p.m. with my neighbors as a thanks to the healthcare workers at shifts' end. I even remember hearing the bus drivers beeping their horns to the 7 p.m. chorus. I can't remember when people started saying "Stay safe, stay well" at the end of a conversation. I do remember how tired everyone looked over the mask, scarves or bandanas.

I had been working after years of underemployment, and that shut down in March of 2020. There was no in-person high school graduation for my son in June of 2020. In November of 2020 my son chose to move out of state. Things were stripped bare, so I was forced to **notice**. Notice the beauty of nature. Notice the grace of people exhausted and taxed beyond all reasonableness. Grace for the folks who couldn't cope with the strain. Grief for those we lost.

Through it all, I leaned on my faith, because I had so little else. I remember going to church when it reopened, all of us sitting distanced, masked. But we were there, however few of us allowed in, we were there. And so was Christ. He was in the eyes of the exhausted EMS workers, He was there with the transit folks, He was in line with us in the rain waiting to get into the supermarket. He was there in the ICUs with the nurses and doctors and the sick. He was there with the birds and the flowers and the flowing Hudson River. He continues to be with us, from now until the end of the world. Enduring the pandemic has been my blessing. A mosaic of Christ's love was created from pain, endurance, kindness, and acceptance.

I am **Julia Hrysenko** and I live in New York City with my partner, pets, and plants. I am a proud mother, classic movie fan, and coffee fiend.

My favorite Bible verse is Psalm 46:10, *"Be still and know that I am God."*

NOEMI'S STORY

Born into a Roman Catholic family, I have been acquainted with Christ my whole life, having been baptized as an infant, receiving the sacraments and married in the Church. However, my relationship with Christ has ebbed and flowed throughout my life, much like a love-not so much love relationship with siblings. Growing up in 1960's Chicago, I attended the local parish Catholic elementary school until my family moved back to Argentina. During those years, I remember wishing that my parents could be more involved in the church community. As recent immigrants to the USA without degrees, their priorities were to work as hard and as much as they could to learn the language and make a living to provide a good life for me and my brother. Unfortunately, that didn't leave much time for many other activities, including attending church regularly or participating in church sponsored activities, but I know they would have if time had permitted.

When we moved to Argentina, my relationship with Christ continued through my continued Catholic education, save for the one year when my parents had sent us to a very elite, exclusive bilingual school, in hopes that we would not lose our English language skills. That experiment did not last long, as I begged my parents to send us to a different school because in my tender 11-year-old heart, I knew that I did not fit in to that privileged world of nannies and chauffeured limousines. Thankfully, my parents acquiesced and my Catholic education continued through the end of grade school, high school, and college, across two continents. The foundation was solidly laid, and it has always served to ground me, reminding me of my deep-rooted faith. Yet life in its infinite twists, turns, and vastness, found ways to test my belief in the subsequent 40 years. Despite all the detours, I have continued to find my way back to Christ.

My first break was when, as newlyweds, no matter how hard we tried, we could not manage to conceive a child. My husband was my rock, but I knew his heart weighed as heavy as mine as we watched one after another of our friends marry and start their families. We smiled and congratulated them, attending baby showers and birthdays while attempting to hide our own sorrow. Each disappointment and month made me question my faith, when, as a teacher within a poor urban area, I watched as so many women who did not seem to have the means to care for their children became pregnant so easily while we who did have the financial means and solid marriage, could not. I drifted from Christ, angry at times, throughout those eight long years. However, it was a tragedy that brought me back to Him when I prayed for a family who had lost their child. I realized then that it was not *our* will, but *His* that would determine a family's future. So I opened my heart to Christ and pledged it to Him, praying that His will be done. One year later, we welcomed our son into our family, and he has been our greatest joy.

When my sister-in-law lost her life in a car crash at the age of 44 and I lost both my mother-in-law and father-in-law within a three-year period, I cried and suffered devastating feelings of loneliness and another loss of faith. I could not understand how the merciful Christ I had always been taught to trust could do something so very hurtful to my husband. But oddly enough, I never asked why. Questioning God was not part of me then nor now.

Life continued with its twists, turns and detours through serious health issues for both my husband and me. He needed and received a kidney transplant through the grace of God in 2016. I say through the grace of God because in his case, I knew that God would protect him. I had absolutely no doubt. Then, at the end of 2017, Christ turned my life completely upside down when I found out I had breast cancer. While most women will cry and rage when learning of their illness, I never did. I never questioned Him or asked why. Because in my heart of hearts, I knew He had chosen me for a reason. Statistics say that one in eight women will be diagnosed with breast cancer in this country. As I looked around to the women in my life, I could not help but thank Christ for choosing me. Because I had faith, I knew He would see me through the most difficult challenge of my life. He was by my side as I underwent 4 rounds of chemo and 33 rounds of radiation. He was with me in my darkest moments of pain, and always with me on my good days. He showed me that I have a very deep reserve of strength and gratitude for all the blessings He has bestowed upon me and continues to give me daily.

When the pandemic hit us in early 2020, my brother and I, along with our spouses, were planning a 60th wedding anniversary celebration for our parents. No one in our family had made it to 60 years of marriage, so we wanted to celebrate our parents for their love and legacy. Their actual anniversary was on March 12, 2020, but the party was scheduled for that Sunday. We had a guest list over 100 people. In the end, the party took place with perhaps 40 people in attendance, as the country and world shut down around us. It was a lovely little celebration, and as I fervently prayed to the Lord, no one in attendance got sick or had any difficulties, just a beautiful memory of a lovely celebration.

Christ has continued to be with me throughout this most trying year, where we remained isolated from family and friends, as He protected my husband from harm given his compromised immunity as a transplant patient. I have learned that even in our darkest moments, Christ will always offer an ember of light to ignite the fire of faith if you remain still enough to let it catch. I learned that distance cannot weaken the bonds of familial love if you work at keeping those bonds tight. Lastly, I was repeatedly reminded that Christ is always with me, in my heart.

———

I am **Noemi Falcone**, also known as Amy or Mimi, and I am a retired Speech-Language Pathologist, breast cancer survivor, and lover of life. Wife to Tom, mother of Michael, and soon to be mother-in-law to Kimmy, I can most often be found in my Connecticut kitchen, making something yummy, or in my favorite chair, giggling while talking to family or friends.

My favorite Bible verse is 1 Corinthians 13:13, *"And now these three remain: faith, hope and love. But the greatest of these is love."*

HARRIET'S STORY

I had a very rough past, one in which abuse and neglect were my constant companions. By today's standards I would have been removed from the dysfunctional family in which I grew up. I went on to live a very self-destructive life, one in which I could have become a statistic because I thought I deserved it. Instead, God saw to it that I met my husband, stayed married for 48 years, had two wonderful children, and four grandchildren.

My life continued like this until Palm Sunday, April 2011, when, sitting with my son in Harvest Bible Church in Illinois, an epiphany occurred. While the pastor was discussing those people who had indeed become statistics, I realized that God had spared me. He had been with me all my life, even though I didn't know He existed. Not only had He been with me and saved me, but He was preparing me for my husband's death the following Sunday on Easter Sunday.

Ten years have passed since I went to Bible study and experienced this epiphany that day in Church. My belief in God as Father and Jesus as Son and Savior has not only strengthened me but has brought people into my life who have helped me survive the internal suffering and emotional pain and trauma. One such person is my psychiatrist, who listened well, understood me completely, and freely gave his empathy and validation to me in our work together for the last seven years. This is how I have come to know Christ and the role He has played in my life.

During the past year I have feared the pandemic, but with God's support it is proving to be temporary and survivable. He has bestowed me with patience, new and meaningful friendships, and a beautiful new place for me to live. At age 84, I didn't think it was possible or that I was even capable of moving to a new home and being able to enjoy my surroundings again. My Lord and Savior Jesus Christ has loved me unconditionally and blessed my family throughout this difficult time. He lives in my heart and has taught me that those who endure to the end will be saved.

I am *Harriet Ayers*, and I live in Spring Meadows, an assisted living facility in Trumbull, Connecticut. I have two adult children, a son in Chicago and a daughter who also lives in Trumbull and is the author of this book. I have been blessed with four wonderful grandchildren who are all teenagers now.

After many years in therapy, actively working to heal from the trauma of childhood abuse, I finally feel well, stable, and am enjoying life. I have made remarkable progress with God's help, and the blessing He sent me in the form of my wonderful doctor for the past seven years. I want you to know it was worth it. Do not give up! I finally have peace of mind in my heart and soul.

My favorite Bible verse is Matthew 24:13, *"Those who endure to the end will be saved."*

SALLY'S STORY

I was raised in a very Catholic family where I was one of my parents' eight children. My father was the main breadwinner, which could be challenging at times. My parents taught us to believe that God would provide every single time, and He did. I also learned at an early age how important it was to have faith and a total belief in God. This lesson has carried me through good and bad times. The year 2020 was a year most of us will never forget. A worldwide pandemic hit and would change our lives forever. Lockdowns, quarantines, hand sanitizers, and surgical masks became a new way of life. In the middle of this stressful time, I received the most wonderful gift I could ever imagine- the gift of a life- saving liver transplant.

I found out that I had liver disease in the summer of 1995. My liver was slowly being damaged by my own immune system. I was able to live a moderately normal life with my husband and four children. I had to rest a lot but was able to keep up with family activities and sports with the kids. In 2019, all of that changed. My liver started to fail, and I started to experience bone weary fatigue. I had to give up most of my daily activities, volunteering, and spending time with friends. As my health declined, my faith grew even stronger.

I've always had a close relationship with God through prayer, but my closeness to Him became unconditional. I knew without a doubt that He would carry me through.

In April of 2019, my health conditional was dire. My liver was dying, and I found out later that I was losing my battle. I was admitted to the hospital on May 2, 2020. That was the day that God started to work miracles. A series of coincidences began to happen. For instance, the nurse walked in after my transfusion and informed me that they wanted me to stay overnight. In the middle of the night, the top transplant surgeon walked in (he just happened to be on duty) and told me that because of the pandemic, several Eastern states had paused their transplant surgeries at the larger hospitals. This part-time delay enabled me to receive a liver from Pittsburgh though we were in Cleveland. The hospital that sent the organ was one that my grandmother had worked at more than 50 years before, and my sister had trained there years ago.

Another coincidence was the timing. My husband is a track coach at the high school level and we always worried that he would have to give up a year of coaching and let the athletes down. However, due to the pandemic, the season was canceled. Finally, because of all the strain and financial burden, I was extremely stressed. He took care of that, too. Our tiny village had fundraisers and neighbors cooked for us for 2 months! We were so humbled and blessed. Again, God did provide. I've made it to my 1-year anniversary, and I feel so lucky and thankful. During one of the deadliest pandemics in our world's history, I was chosen by God to receive the most precious of all gifts, the gift of life.

My name is **Sally Hribar** and I am a mom of four and grandma to eight. My husband and I were high school sweethearts and have been married for forty-one years. We live in Fairport Harbor, Ohio, along the shore of Lake Erie.

My favorite Bible verse is Ecclesiastes 3: 1-2, *"There is a time for everything, and a season for every activity under the heavens...."*

SONYA'S STORY

Both of my parents were raised as traditional southern Baptists. I was born and raised in Northeastern Ohio, and we used to go on summer vacations to North Carolina and Georgia, the states where my parents were born and raised. Attending primitive Baptist church in North Carolina and Georgia was different than attending the same denomination church in Ohio. My experience in Ohio as a Baptist was a little more contained than how my parents were raised. By that I mean it wasn't so "holy-roly." While you could feel the Spirit during church you didn't have people jumping up and screaming because they felt the Holy-Ghost. Looking back at my childhood experience, I was afraid, and didn't understand what was happening. In my home church in Ohio, God's presence was there, but the congregation's response was a little more subdued. Yes, you would hear a lot of "Amens," but generally, folks didn't just jump straight up out of their pews because they literally felt the Holy-Spirit.

I was a young adult in college when my father retired and became a deacon at the local Baptist church. My mother didn't enjoy the local Baptist church so she started studying with a group of Jehovah's Witness women that would come by the house. I was split. I went to church with my father and attended assemblies with my mother. It was a surreal experience as I reflect, because I didn't judge either one of them. I think at that point in my life I admired them for doing their "own" thing by being engaged with God through each one of their select religions. Each respected the other, and my mother would still participate in church activities and bake cakes for events at my father's church. Looking back, I don't believe my father ever participated in any Jehovah's Witness activities, but he didn't discourage or put my mother down for her choice of devotion either. He always happily greeted the women visiting with respect. I share this story because it adds to the complexity of my journey with Christ, where it began, and how I continue to grow in my love for Him. My parents' relationship with God and how they worshipped would play a pivotal role in a major decision that I would make much later in my life.

I met a man who was devoted to Christ. He attended and graduated from religiously focused college and law school and went to church every Sunday for worship. He loved the Lord, but he was Catholic and I was Baptist. While we worshipped the same God, the Father of Abraham, our religions and our Christ-led journey couldn't have been more different.

I was baptized when I was an adult, not as a child. This is a huge difference between Baptists and Catholics. My parents' decision on religion was that each child would choose for themselves. I ultimately selected the Baptist religion and became baptized as an adult.

When my husband asked me to marry him, we talked about our different religions, prayed about it, and asked ourselves, "How would it work?" We knew that God wanted us to worship Him as a family, not separately, and that we wanted to be truly seen as one in His eyes as we continued our journey of faith. I thought about my parents so many years earlier and how they worshipped the Lord separately. This was so important to both my future husband and me that we wanted to devote our family to one religion. I converted to Catholicism and my husband was my sponsor. We both went through a pretty rigorous program called RCIA (Rite of Christian Initiation of Adults) because we were both committed. It was a beautiful journey that we experienced together.

It didn't matter that I started my journey experiencing two different religions, choosing one and then converting to another. Christ is so much bigger than any religion. My journey in knowing Christ has never been a straight road, and I continue to take twists and turns. My prayer is that I continue to have God as the focus, guiding me along the road, and ultimately kneeling before Him.

There have been some major stormy seasons in my life that Christ has protected and carried me through. Some have brought rainbows and sunshine, but still in some there are clouds. As Paul teaches us in Philippians 4:11-13, *"I am not saying this because I am in need, for I have learned to be content whatever the circumstances. I know what it is to be in need, and I know what it is to have plenty. I have learned the secret of being content in any and every situation, whether well fed or hungry, whether living in plenty or in want. I can do all this through Him who gives me strength."*

I have learned that it is right to be content regardless of the situation, but it is still a struggle at times. Death, sickness, chronic illnesses, broken relationships and lost jobs have all brought me to my knees in prayer, sometimes to praise God, and yes, sometimes to scream at God, too. When these times hit, I rely on the verse Romans 8:28, *"And we know that in all things God works for the good of those who love him, who have been called according to his purpose."* I adopted this verse as my life's guidance more than twenty years ago, and it is still relevant to me today. God's mercies are new every day, and it proves that while life happens, His word never changes.

I know that I can do all things through Him who strengthens me, though that doesn't necessarily make it any easier. However, it does help to carry me through because I know that the Lord's got me literally in His arms, carrying me through whatever storm is trying to blow me down. For me, believing in God the Father, the Son, and the Holy Spirit, truly gives me hope. It gives me hope that there will be a rainbow, a ray of sunshine on the other side. Even if there are clouds showing me that there is a storm brewing, I must stand firm, have faith, and know that that is okay, too. I trust in the Lord that He will bring me through my sorrow, my pain, my anger, and ultimately my disappointment.

I acknowledge that the pandemic has been horrible for me

and the rest of the world. In this situation, I can honestly say that misery doesn't love company. What the world has been walking through, I wish on no one. The fact that everyone is walking through the same fire doesn't really make me feel any better. I recently read a piece online on Holy Bible You Version that touched my heart, "I declare that you are blessed every day of your life and you lack nothing. I pray that as you walk through the storm the waves will not swallow you and that the winds will not knock you down. I pray that God's goodness, favor and mercy shall pursue you, overtake you and cover you all the days of your life. In Jesus's Name, Amen." What a message to embrace during this pandemic! The global pandemic was a storm that the entire world was fighting at the same time. The novel COVID-19 virus brought tremendous challenges, but it also brought tremendous blessings.

The season has been long living with COVID-19, and the blessings that I have experienced have come in stages. I believe that these stages contributed to my growth as a person who loves the Lord. Being "locked-in" allowed me to find quiet time and evaluate if and how I reflect God in my life. Six stages of blessings that helped me grow during the pandemic consist of:

Fear - The pandemic killed so many people and no one knew what to do. My family, like many, were afraid. The Catholic hymn that popped into my head to meditate on during the beginning of COVID-19 was by John Michael Talbot, Be Not Afraid.

Be not afraid
I go before you always.
Come, follow me and I will give you rest

Resiliency - Both my husband and I are strategists, so we applied strategy to keep our family safe, and came up with a safety plan that we implemented throughout COVID-19. We still have rules even though the pandemic is winding down.

Appreciation - I have always had the utmost appreciation for my family and friends, but now I had an enhanced appreciation for the front-line workers and the families of those who died from the virus, and I actively pray for them and our government officials. I was not doing this before.

Reflection - Forced alone time gave each of us the opportunity to reflect and look in the mirror. It's a chance that many of us don't want to take advantage of, and COVID-19 made me self-evaluate and take much needed time for reflection.

Empathy – Through reflection, one clear virtue that was missing in me, and in my life, was empathy. I had to fall to my knees and admit that I am not as empathetic as I should be, and this is an area that God revealed to me that I need to work on.

True gratefulness – I thought I knew about gratefulness. Although it has visited me so often in my life, true gratitude is bigger than life. I can now say that I have experienced the fullness of God's grace through my pandemic blessings.

The blessings that I experienced came from personal growth. God worked on me during this period, and He used fear to help me gain resilience, which fueled appreciation. My appreciation allowed me to reflect on who I am and forced me to admit my inadequacy in the area of empathy which finally pushed me to the final stage of embracing true gratefulness.

My prayer for all of us is that we do not forget this COVID-19 season; that we take what we learned and receive all of the pandemic blessings in their fullness to glorify God, the Father, the Son and the Holy Spirit. Amen.

I am **Sonya Ruff Jarvis** and I have been a corporate executive, Bible study teacher, organizer of events with tens of thousands of attendees, and now a successful small business owner. Through all of this, I have run the New York City Marathon, survived breast cancer, and created an innovative business-to-business customer relationship model. My husband, Scott and I live in Connecticut with our daughter, Sara, who is a fierce athlete, and our Havanese dog, Sadie, who completes our family.

My favorite Bible verse is Romans 8:28, *"And we know that in all things God works for the good of those who love him, who have been called according to his purpose."*

RENEE'S STORY

I first came to know who Christ was as a child. However, our family was not religious by any means. I can recall starting to frequent church more when I was in middle school and high school. There were droves of teens who would walk to our Catholic church for Saturday evening service, but it felt more like a social obligation instead of a working relationship. My parents divorced a few years later, and I ended up moving to another town to live with my dad and his girlfriend who was now my stepmother. At the time, my grandmother didn't care for my dad's girlfriend because "she's a Baptist" and "not like us." I really didn't know the difference but thought that my stepmom was nice enough.

My relationship with my parents was more of a friendship. My brother and I were born to teen parents who basically grew up with us. We had a tumultuous childhood, and the only continuity we had was with our friends in our small town. I felt like my biggest role models were teachers or other adults in the neighborhood. My parents, each pointing the finger of blame at each other, still cannot get along to this day despite getting divorced almost 40 years ago.

After I graduated high school, I went away to college and

still occasionally went to the weekly "religious" service on campus. I felt like most church services were more ritualistic, and that I just needed to stand, kneel, and say things at the right moment. Therefore, I never felt a strong bond to Christ. I chose a career in law enforcement and only went to church for obligatory reasons such as for weddings, funerals, Christmas, and Easter. I married a fellow police officer in 1993 and we traveled extensively, worked hard, and played harder. Most of our friends were police officers, too, and my life was fun, but it was one-dimensional. I lost a baby at 5 months of pregnancy when I was almost 35, and I can only recall praying for her health. I never prayed to thank God for all he'd given me and only prayed to ask for the things I wanted or needed to be done.

Shortly thereafter, I realized that my marriage didn't feel right and that my husband was solely focused on work and his promotions. I divorced him in 2003 and moved back to my hometown, to a small apartment. By that time, I had been promoted to detective and was assigned to SVU, mostly dealing with sexual assault cases. I began to utilize very unhealthy coping mechanisms, including binge drinking. Although I didn't have a relationship with Christ then, He was certainly protecting me as well as other people on the road. This pattern continued for 2-3 years, until I met my current husband. He was a believer in Christ, but clearly had backslid. He also didn't drink, which eventually taught me that I didn't need to drink to deal with my problems either.

He was in school for his doctorate, so I still had free time to begin considering retiring at 20 years in law enforcement and pursuing a second career. Right around this time, I also disclosed to a victim's aunt how I'd been repeatedly molested as a child, by someone who married into our family. I think it started off as my attempting to console this woman because she felt guilty, like she hadn't been able to protect her niece from being molested. This is when I really needed a healthy coping mechanism, and my future husband was a great source of support. However, he also had many stressors, financial and otherwise.

I had an orthopedic surgery in 2007 and came to realize that I depended on Ambien in order to sleep at night. In May of 2008, frustrated with the weight of the world and not wanting to cope with alcohol, I ended up taking a handful of Ambien one night. I believe I wanted to just rest and deal with my problems at some later time. I don't remember wanting to die. I just wanted to escape all the thoughts, emotions, and hopelessness that seemed so prevalent during that time. Thankfully, I reached out to a friend, who called 911. The next day, two of my friends witnessed to me, and I began to read the Bible. I didn't feel at home in the few churches I visited. Although life felt better, I still hadn't learned how to cope.

I began therapy for PTSD, related to finally unpacking the baggage of the molestation, and began training for an endurance event, the century bike ride. I worked with my therapist and was going to begin EMDR (Eye Movement Desensitization and Reprocessing therapy) to more fully address and heal my trauma, but in early March of 2009, I found out I was pregnant. My therapist was afraid that EMDR would be very traumatic, and she didn't want me to risk losing the baby especially because I'd lost one seven years earlier. My husband graduated from his doctorate program that May, and in November, my daughter was born. I honestly feel like God gave her to us in order for us to return to Him.

When my daughter was 3 months old, I began taking her to my stepmom's church. My husband saw immediate changes in my attitude, and about a month after I started going to church and bible study, he began coming, too! It was then that I realized that, while I do believe in therapy for mental health issues, I really needed more Christ in my life. God restored our relationship, and plays a huge role in my life, our marriage, and our family. He is our provider, our strength, our hope, and our role model. He is our decision maker, our forgiver, and our entire identity. My husband and I have struggles, some similar and some different, and we feel that the only way to overcome them is through a relationship with Christ and constant communication with Him.

I took a leap of faith in 2008 and went back to school for nursing. The twenty-month program began when our daughter was twenty-two months old. My husband was out-of-state visiting with my two stepsons every other weekend and was also working two jobs. I was still working part time, and my father was diagnosed with cancer shortly after I started nursing school. His medical team performed surgery for his cancer one year later in my second year of school. Statistically, one-third of my classmates failed along the way, but I graduated! I know it was only possible because it was His will and plan for me to serve him now as a Registered Nurse.

Considering the COVID-19 pandemic, I have been much less focused on the cares and struggles of the world, primarily because of my faith and partially because I began a new position just before the pandemic hit. When I'm at work, my mind is focused on how to best serve my organization and Christ. I've become far more removed from politics because most discussions about politics result in arguing. I've been focused on displaying the love of Christ and working for Him. Most of my coworkers have teleworked for nearly a year, so I really needed to rely on Christ for direction when I was trying to learn my new role. I had to display humility when I didn't know how to perform specific tasks, and when I had to ask for help. I've worked on my patience and self-control, realizing that these were areas that I needed to work on. And when I stumble, He convicts me with love and is ready to forgive.

I've had family members who had Covid, and I've sadly also lost a few friends to it. My focus during the pandemic was to spread the gospel through words and actions, especially when He led me to the unsaved. I think some of the biggest blessings during Covid were spending more time with my family and still being able to attend church, online for ten weeks, outdoors for over four months, and in person for the last seven months and counting. I don't feel like I'm rushing around as much, and we were blessed with having our daughter in school for the entire school year. Most importantly, my church and biological family have all survived, even though some did come down with Covid. It has also taught me obedience to the authority ordained by God, realizing that He is in control of all things. His mercies are new each and every morning. We must all learn from our sins but not dwell on them. All glory to God for being the only thing that can change us.

———◆—————

I am **Renee Sheckfee,** and I am eternally grateful for second chances, and for Christ having blessed me with a Godly husband, beautiful daughter, sweet stepsons, and for placing me in careers serving others, to witness for Christ.

My favorite Bible verse is Romans 15:5-6, *"May the God who gives endurance and encouragement give you the same attitude of mind toward each other that Christ Jesus had, so that with one mind and one voice you may glorify the God and Father of our Lord Jesus Christ."*

LILLY'S STORY

When I look back and consider the question of how I came to know Christ, I realize that I had been wanting to come to Christ for a long time but had never had anyone to really explain how to go about it. It's ironic, as I was raised as a Catholic and went to Catholic school, but I only did as I was told and unfortunately never really understood God, Jesus, and the Holy Spirit. There was always a huge Bible on top of my mother's dresser, opened and with a rosary made from wood. Yet, I never saw my mother, or anyone for that fact, read it. We were not even allowed to touch it, and as far as I was concerned or had been taught, only the priests in church were allowed to do so.

I never read the Bible at home, and religious classes were taught without any of us touching or reading from a Bible. This all confirmed for me that we were prohibited. However, I was always interested in learning what the Bible was about. I often asked questions, especially when learning about Paul and Peter. Still, no one sat with me or taught me that I too could read the Bible.

While attending a public high school, I took a religious class and learned a little about other religions, which I found fascinating. I would discuss it with my mom, and she would reply, "that's great that you are learning, but we are Catholics." Again, no one sat with me to explain, and no Bible reading was allowed. I remained under the impression that it was a book only for priests and was meant to be placed on top of a dresser.

As I continued to college, I found that God has ways to speak to us even when we do not know how to speak with Him. A friend of mine invited me to his home and upon arrival I saw a black leather book on the end table. Being curious, I asked about it. He answered me in a surprised manner, simply stating "It's the Bible." I was taken aback. It was on a table, not untouchable on top of a dresser. I thought to myself, "his mother and family actually read from it? What kind of Bible was it?" My friend bought me my first Bible for Christmas that year. I cried, but sadly, could not read it because it was in the old KJV version. It didn't matter though, because what was important and amazing to me was that I now had my own Bible!

Moving forward a few years, I married a man whose family was Pentecostal. God has ways that we do not understand. My sister-in-law took our daughter to church, but I wouldn't join. I was Catholic, and that was the only religion I knew. My father-in-law soon had a sit-down discussion with me, and I ended up attending Sunday school for the first time. It was a revelation to me that someone was finally teaching me the Word of God, and I was amazed and humbled. I accepted Jesus Christ into my life in 1989, and although it has not always been easy, it has been the most important decision of my life. I have been serving Him for over 30 years, I was anointed a Children's Pastor, and I am currently an Associate Pastor in my church. I continue to seek His presence and will in all areas of my life.

My faith was tested when we were hit with COVID-19 in March of 2020. I could not believe it was happening in the United States! Our Pastor had been telling us months prior to the pandemic that we should be prepared because something was going to affect our country. We held a prepping class and I started buying extra food and other essentials, but I was not scared or worried. Within weeks, the news showed everything shutting down, and people began dying, first in other parts of the world and then in our own world and communities. Stores were running out of essentials for the first time, and toilet paper and other cleaning products were being rationed. I increased my prayers and started speaking to family and friends who were not attending church or had left, saying that this is a time for us to reflect on who we are in Christ and what are we doing with our lives.

Our church had to close its doors, but I asked God to help me find a way to continue teaching His Word, and He did just that. I opened a women's online Bible Study in both English and Spanish, as well as opened Sunday school and church midweek for children. In fact, I had children sharing their reflections on Bible lessons and youth worshipping online. We held our discipleship classes online, and we never stopped ministering, praying, or helping others. We figured out how to store food in our church by converting a closet into a pantry and have been feeding families ever since. We were able to provide food, clothing, and whatever else we could offer to help families. It has been extraordinary and fulfilling to know that God has given us the strength, creativity, and resources needed to support families in need.

The pandemic enabled me to see what God had been birthing within my spirit. My Bible studies increased, my teachings increased, and I have learned and continue to learn how to depend completely on my God for all my needs. I became more compassionate and reached out for help when I needed it. I love what God has been doing in me, and I am beyond grateful for this process.

I am glad to see that the death toll and the COVID cases are decreasing with the onset of vaccinations. I still cannot believe how many have tragically passed away, and I continually pray for their families. Watching the news, I didn't care about politics, but rather wanted only facts, truth, and God. This pandemic indeed brought me closer to Christ, helped me to grow even more spiritually, and helped me to do even more for others for the Glory of God.

———————

I am *Lilly Rios*, married with two grown children, and soon to be a first-time grandmother. I'm a retired Connecticut special education teacher, and currently a children's Pastor and women's ministry leader.

My favorite Bible verse is Psalm 139: 1-6, *"O LORD, you have searched me and known me! You know when I sit down and when I rise up; You discern my thoughts from afar. You search out my path and my lying down and are acquainted with all my ways. Even before a word is on my tongue, behold, O LORD, you know it altogether. You hem me in, behind and before, and lay your hand upon me. Such knowledge is too wonderful for me, it is high; I cannot attain it."*

EVELYS'S STORY

Thirteen going on thirty. Not the movie, but the cinematic movie version that sums up my own life. As I child, I would attend church services with my paternal aunt, but my parents didn't go with me. I knew what church was, but I didn't build a relationship with Christ until the age of 13. Our walk with Christ sometimes seems more like a race, and may involve other people to plant the seed, but it is an ultimately individual process by the time it begins to grow. This happened for me at the time when I realized the emptiness I felt, even though I was surrounded by others. I didn't know what would come next, but I knew I would no longer feel alone as long as I had the Holy Spirit with me.

During my teen years. I became involved with various ministries at my church which included youth ministry, singing, dancing, Missionettes, and other programs. I vowed that my testimony would impact other girls, and that I would remain pure, holy, and love on others. As we know, the teenage years make you dream and strive for greatness, but they have their ups and downs as well. I remained faithful to God, but I struggled to face myself as my life became busy. I forgot to let God deal with areas in which I needed help, and when people let me down, I began to struggle with depression and anxiety. I knew of God and Jesus, and I would write down my prayers, praise, and worship honestly, but I didn't allow them to work for me because I wanted it my way and in my timing.

When I entered my college years, it became harder to fight these battles. The years of 18-23 were like a wild roller coaster in which I encountered years of spiritual impact that was life changing. I began to see I needed to build a personal relationship with God. I stopped going to church and then would start up again, until I finally learned how to grow in my walk of faith. I learned to listen to God rather than allow my prayers to become a one-way conversation. I learned that He had so much more for me than just what was inside the four walls of a building.

During this young adult period, I had definitely matured, but in some areas I was still a child. I was trying to be "perfect" and not let anyone see my weaknesses or failures, which isn't how Jesus asked us to live life. I met my husband around my mid-twenties, and this relationship helped me to mature individually and spiritually. It brought up many aspects of myself that I knew I had to work on. My life felt like a semi-façade because I had never dealt with my feelings and emotions appropriately. I had learned to suppress them to be a people pleaser, and it was slowly killing me. At this time, I had to unlearn habits that were hurting me and realize it was okay to break down in the arms of God to allow Him to rebuild those areas. I had to learn to be vulnerable, honest, open, and trusting. This was what I needed to do for God before I could do it with people who surrounded me and loved me.

Walls broke down, and I was being filled little by little. I was making an effort. Jesus gave me friends who are like sisters, a ministry to lead, and a home. My depression during college had to be dealt with, but that final breakthrough didn't happen until I reached my 30s. I allowed God to help with some parts of my life, but not yet with everything.

Finally, when I was enjoying my marriage, learning, and laughing, a personal and deeply painful roadblock occurred in my life. For someone who had a wonderful childhood, I wasn't truly prepared to deal with that much change and heartbreak all at once. These past 5 years have been the most impactful of my life in so many ways. I felt my body was betraying me. I was always tired, in pain, and struggling to have a baby. My maternal grandmother suddenly passed away, and the following year, my paternal grandmother also passed away without warning. These women helped raise me, and I lost them both. My family turned their backs on me, my parents, and my brother, and our family holidays came to an end.

I ended up in the hospital several times because of my kidneys and had to go through several medical procedures to find out I had Endometriosis. I was trying to go through the IVF (In Vitro Fertilization) process. It was a challenging and difficult process both physically and emotionally. I felt myself slipping away, becoming numb to bad news, jealous of other women getting pregnant, and angry because my grandmothers never had the chance to meet my future children. The COVID-19 pandemic felt like a sign of the end of times, and people didn't know what to expect. Depression started setting in once again.

Just like before, I didn't want to let God in when it came to my depression. For whatever reason, I thought I could handle it on my own, but ended up making my situation worse for myself. With so much happening all at once, I became angry with God and blamed him for not doing what I wanted when I wanted it. During 2019-2020, I went through a personal battle when I finally admitted I was not okay and needed help. At that point, my healing began. The pandemic helped me to finally face myself, my losses, and my emotional pain. I prayed, screamed, cried, smiled, and worshipped all through the pain and grief. All God wanted me to do is surrender the pain that didn't belong to me, to be real with Him and know that He is God, not me. He wants to fight my battles.

As 2020 turned to 2021, I miraculously began to overcome the depression that I had struggled with for so long. I prayed fervently, telling God that I didn't want to waste another year fighting the same battles and taking what the enemy meant for evil, without allowing God to turn it for good. I asked the Lord to let me continue to grow, use me to bless others, and let my life and testimony be evidence of what He can do in someone's life. That's exactly what has been happening. I am trusting God like never before because I know He is real and has the best intentions for my life. Life will never be perfect because we are imperfect beings, but I serve a God that makes the impossible indeed possible. 35 until forever, here I come.

—————— ◆ ——————

I am **Evelys Rios-Lopez**, and I currently live in Connecticut with my husband and dog. I am a special education teacher working in a public high school. I enjoy traveling, food tours with friends, and relaxing at home. I have been a believer of Christ since the age of 13.

My favorite Bible verse is John 4:22-24, *"You worship what you do not know; we worship what we know, for salvation is from the Jews. But the hour is coming, and is now here, when the true worshippers will worship the Father in spirit and truth, for the Father is seeking such people to worship him. God is spirit, and those who worship him must worship in spirit and truth."*

Pandemic Blessings: Stories of Thanksgiving in an Unusual Time

54

ROXANNE'S STORY

I was very fortunate growing up, in that I was raised in a Christian home. My grandmother had a relationship with the Lord that was strong and real. She brought that experience with God into every aspect of her life, which included raising me. You may ask, "Well, what does that look like?" That meant she had scripture to back up her day-to-day life of making right choices. In most homes we are taught right from wrong. The twist in my home was, in addition to being taught good morals, you were taught Bible verses to solidify why something was the right course of action.

Let me give you an example: I was about eight years old, and I decided I was going to steal a dollar out of my Grandma's purse. After having stolen the money, I was riddled with guilt and confessed. Most parents would have stated it was wrong what you did and then would have you promise to not do it again. My grandmother did say that, but then had me go to the Ten Commandments in Exodus to read the one pertaining to stealing. We then knelt down together to pray for forgiveness from God because I had broken one of the commandments. Because she always portrayed God as a

God of love and forgiveness, I was never afraid to tell God when I messed up.

Despite my upbringing, when I started college, I began to stray from my relationship with God. By the time I graduated from college and moved to my own apartment, I stopped attending church and no longer had personal devotional time with the Lord. This lasted about two years. I remember one night having a dream where there was a giant clock that followed me wherever I went. It seemed, in the dream, that I couldn't get away from that clock. It caused me to feel anxious that I was running out of time. When I awoke, I was struck by the overwhelming feeling that time was short. That dream stayed with me for a while. I went on with my life, not giving my relationship with God, or lack of one, much thought.

That summer, the end of my two-year period not attending church, I went on vacation to Hawaii. While there, I went to a beach that was gorgeous. From one vantage point you could see mountains in the distance and huge boulders lining the edges of the beach. If that wasn't enough, whenever the waves would wash up on the shore, there was this melodic, tinkling sound. I had never heard that before or since. I was told that the sound was due to small pebbles on the beach floor that, when having rolled due to the rush of the water, made that beautiful sound. The amazing beauty of this scene struck me profoundly. The only response that I could utter was "How Great Thou Art!" Oddly enough, my dream that I had had so long ago, came to mind at that moment, too. It was almost like an epiphany. The Lord was calling me back to Him. I was wasting precious time that could be used to build our wonderful and precious relationship.

I returned to Connecticut after my Hawaii trip and knew I wanted to rededicate myself to God. I started going back to church and then got re-baptized at a beach in Brooklyn. I started getting involved with the youth in my church, and God used me well in this ministry. He showed me how to be bold for Him, and because of that, I encountered many faith building experiences. God is teaching me how to rely on His strength and how to rest in Him. What could have been a life fraught with anxiety was replaced with a life to which God freely granted peace and security. He is my Rock and high tower.

Then the pandemic really took the world by surprise. Thankfully, because of the faithfulness of God, I never worried about my welfare or that of my family. I knew God would protect and keep us through it all. Instead, He also took us on a big adventure. It was during the pandemic that God led us to sell both of our homes and to move to New Hampshire. He was so clear that this was His will for us, it was hard to not be obedient. We sold both houses in nine days each and were able to get full asking price for both homes. I questioned why God chose for us to move to that area. We looked at properties in New Hampshire, Vermont, and Maine. My husband always dreamed about living in New Hampshire, but it was clear this was God leading us. I have learned from experience that when you ask God for reasons,

He will answer you. The answer for why He led us to this part of the country is because these three states are the most secular in all the United States. There is no house of worship, for my religion, closer than an hour away. I now know that God wants us to shine for Him in this part of our country. I have surrendered my life to God, so He can use me for His glory.

I am **Roxanne August**, and I was born and grew up in New York City. I moved to Connecticut, where I was a special education teacher for 31 years. I currently live in New Hampshire with my husband and daughter. As an active member of my church, I was blessed to organize two mission trips to Central and South America to help build a school and renovate a church.

My favorite Bible verse is John 16:33, *"I have said these things to you, that in me you may have peace. In the world you will have tribulation. But take heart; I have overcome the world."*

JONETTE'S STORY

Amid all the chaos this life tends to bring, I am honored to serve a good God who supplies all my needs and more. As a Christian, I love that I can learn from my past, let it go, take hold of what is in front of me, and have hope for the future. I have been blessed to know my Lord and Savior since I was a young child, when my parents started taking me to church and living out their Christian life with my two siblings. I know at times I take those experiences for granted, as I was able to learn of God's love and hope since I began to understand other truths about this world. Unfortunately, my family life wasn't always happy, and my parents divorced when I was about twelve years old. The shaky foundation began to give way.

Despite the challenges of a family divorce and trying to figure myself out as a young teenager, I was appreciative of the solid ground that the Heavenly Father's love and truths were already stirring within me. My faith has always been a large part of my life, despite selfishness and defiance creeping in at times. Overall, I am thankful for the foundation of my faith, and grateful to all those who helped instill that in me. Life here on Earth is great but difficult, joyful yet sad, defeating yet hopeful, and so I reach towards my Heavenly Father to receive his calm and comforting peace.

Living a life of Christ in this world can be hard, and although ultimately rewarding, it can be hard to see beyond the difficulty to that reward. My life has taken many turns, especially when I was a teenager, and my family began to tear apart. I often found myself feeling lost, confused, and hurt. There were many times in which I felt I was at a crossroads, and sometimes I made choices I am not proud of. Yet, God was always willing to bring me back when I sought Him and asked. He is a graceful and forgiving God, and I am so thankful for that. I searched for Him when I was young, and I searched as I got older, for His guidance in all things from my schooling, relationships, and career, to starting a family of my own. He has not failed me once, and although I didn't see it this way every time, like a prayer falling on deaf ears, He was listening. His ways are higher than our ways.

This past year has been a roller coaster of new events, emotions, and everything in between. With the pandemic, a new reality dawned, with some changes that have made life more difficult than ever before. This year has brought me to seek and become closer to my Savior than ever, because of the uncertainty of it all. In the beginning of the pandemic, I was admittedly pushing back on all the new rules and restrictions, though a time came when I finally had to give in and stop resisting. It was then that the Lord began to work in me, giving me peace and blessing on what was to come.

My children, a four-year-old son and two-year-old daughter, who had just begun a healthy, structured routine at an early learning center, were now back at home with me and my husband, and we were teleworking through it all. As a therapist who thrives and depends on the "personability" of my work, this brought new challenges to the therapeutic relationship and progress. The background noise and interruptions from my children playing started off as a nuisance and something I tried to hide, but as time went on I began to recognize it as a blessing to hear them play and laugh in the safety of our home and be able to spend more time with them during the day. The hour-long commute turned into a 3 second walk to the family room. The dinners shared weren't rushed into bedtime routines. The workouts in the morning were allowed to start a little later, and more sleep is always a blessing in my eyes. The afternoon drives to pick up food were a nice get away and a time to talk and share our thoughts and plans. I looked forward to these trips to get something to eat and gradually head back home. The neighborhood walks with kids in the wagon on a breezy afternoon allowed more time to share and spend with one another. The essence of time and togetherness was being woven together as it always should have been.

The challenges and barriers of this pandemic became the topic of many sessions, stemming from the impact on our everyday lives, and allowed for a greater degree of relatability and genuine concern for one another. We rode the waves of uncertainty together and came up with positives with which we could all identify. The hope of it all getting better was based in my faith, and that is where I allowed my fear to remain in the hands of my Heavenly Father.

Amongst the changes with work, my family was in for the biggest change of all. This time at home gave my husband and I time to think, talk and pray, leading us to our next mission in life, to foster children and hopefully one day adopt them into our own family. This took a lot more prayer and inner change because it was a new idea, a foreseeable challenge, and quite the turn-around from all I had planned previously. But God is a good God and knows all, and He began to change my heart on this issue. At the start of the pandemic, we began to seek out a faith based foster agency and moved forward. The pandemic allowed us to get all our training and requirements done on live video, which allowed the entry process to be smooth and even convenient. As 2020 turned to 2021, and while the pandemic still raged on, our family began to foster 3 beautiful children. The blessing that God has given us, we will also share with them as we are preparing our future to include and adopt them as our own. Similar to the pains of childbirth, the challenges of this pandemic have been many and difficult, yet God intends good. Following His will allows us to birth new beginnings and reap new blessings. Praise God!

I am *Jonette Lucio*, and I live in Texas with my wonderful husband, two beautiful biological children, and three sweet foster siblings. I am honored to work as a licensed counselor specializing in the needs of teenager and young adult issues, as my calling is to help those who are hurting and in need. My Christian faith is very important to me and my family, as we love God and love to have fun as a family, whether it's out on the beach, on the playground, or going for a nice drive out of town.

My favorite Bible verse is Proverbs 3: 5-6, *"Trust in the Lord will all your heart and lean not on your own understanding; in all your ways submit to Him, and He will make your paths straight."*

STACEY'S STORY

I am still coming to know Christ after many years. I grew up in what you could call a Christian environment but had no real understanding of what a relationship with Jesus meant. I went to church when I was a child and was sent to a Christian school from kindergarten to 12th grade. The Gospel message surrounded me, but it was white noise, like a TV that's constantly on in the background. My parents were professing Christians but were troubled people. My father, a teacher, spent most of his free time away from home. The time he spent away grew as the years passed until he was spending every weekend in New York, and summers away on vacations. My mom was understandably depressed, and her depression expressed itself in anger at my dad. Their relationship was a Cold War, constant hostility but never divorce.

My older sister and I had very different personalities and did not get along very well. She was much more confident than I was, at least on the outside, and thought I was "weird." I sided with my mom against my dad in their strife, feeling that he had abandoned her and did not love her as I did. I pushed away the God I thought they represented, thinking He did not like women and wanted to subjugate them to men, whom I found very hard to trust. I did not feel comfortable at my Christian school or at church, which I stopped going to for years. I was resentful of God and afraid of Him, but felt I was unable to stand up under what I believed would be mountains of shame crashing down on me if I approached Him.

Years later, after college, coming back to church, and living a nominal "Christian" life in which I felt a little safer than I had in the rest of the world, I went through a series of upending life experiences. From losing my job, losing my apartment, getting into a first, brief, chaotic relationship with a man and getting pregnant, and then losing my baby. It would take too long to tell you all the ways that God surrounded me in those times, and all of the people of his that showed up to help me. Everyone at church, my boss at my retail job, the career counselor I visited when I was pregnant, and even the nurse who stayed overnight in the hospital when I lost my baby, just to be there for me.

In the following weeks and months, I was consumed with terror. I could not eat, sleep, or be alone comfortably. I knew in my bones that I was not going to heaven. I believed in Jesus but did not love him like people around me did. I didn't want to go to hell, but neither did I want to admit to being a terrible, awful person. I couldn't allow God to shame me and change everything about myself. That's what I imagined repentance was like. I was afraid of hell, but also afraid of God.

One of the God-sent people I met was a counselor. When I saw her the first time, something inside me believed I could trust her, and I told her my whole story, including my fears of hell and of God. When I was done, she told me it was strange that my case had been assigned to her, because she was the only born-again Christian in the facility, as far as she knew. It took me a very long time to step closer to God. My counselor and I began to talk about someone I called Not-Scary Jesus. I would imagine Not-Scary Jesus sitting on the couch with me. I would imagine him accepting all the different parts of me, as though they were people invited to his table. My counselor told me that, to Jesus, I was like the pile of tangled gold chains in her jewelry box. You had to take your time to untangle them without breaking them, but you did it because they were precious, and you wanted to wear them. All my doubts, confusion, defenses, and wrong beliefs were parts of myself that were tangled up, but Jesus was taking his time to carefully untangle them, because I was precious to him.

When the pandemic and the eventual lockdown began, I hoped in my heart that Not-Scary Jesus wanted to spend time alone with me, to be with me. I had decided that I would try to read the Gospels for myself and try to get to know Jesus through them. My church had begun online services. At one of them, the pastor asked if anyone wanted to commit their life to Jesus, they could click a button. I was immediately afraid. I did not want to have to answer a ton of questions or explain things, but when I clicked the button, I also felt a strong sense of relief. No one asked me anything, or "outed" me, but after I clicked, I could see another click. And another. And another. Afterwards, I went to my room, and there was a text from the pastor saying that he had been praying for me.

I still fail, and I still struggle with tangled fears, doubts, and unbelief. However, I try to take baby steps. One of them has been honesty with some of my Christian friends about where I've been and what I've felt, which has helped to free me from guilt and pretense. People have messaged me at random times saying that they were praying for me and offering words of encouragement. Never anyone I would have expected, but that makes it more of a blessing. I know I didn't ask for it and God must have nudged them to reach out to me. I am thankful to God for his patience with me. My pride, fears, and doubts have not driven him away.

Sometimes I feel like I am one of the kids I work with as a teacher's aide, helping children with special needs. I picture Jesus is quietly in the school hallway with me, waiting for me to be ready to go into the classroom, but not leaving me alone. Last spring during lockdown, I was walking outside and saw the underbelly of a red-tailed hawk flying overhead, surprisingly close. There was a big stick in her mouth; she must have been building a nest. I began looking for her whenever I walked, hoping to catch a glimpse of the nest. One day, I heard those sharp cries and looked into the sky. There were not one, but three hawks soaring in a circle. Right away I thought Father, Son, and Holy Spirit. I write this to feed the part of me that believes that God sees me, loves me, and has not abandoned me, even in the midst of my doubts.

I am **Stacey Tuhey**, and I am an elementary school paraeducator, living in Connecticut with my mom and our cat, Gigi.

One of my favorite Bible verses is 1 John 3:19-22, *"This is how that we belong to the truth and how we set our hearts at rest in his presence. If our hearts condemn us, we know that God is greater than our hearts, and he knows everything. Dear friends, if our hearts do not condemn us, we have confidence before God and receive from him anything we ask, because we keep his commands and do what pleases him."*

AMBER'S STORY

As a child, I first came to know Christ while I was a member of the Catholic Church, which to me meant that I didn't feel I got to know Him very well at all. I was so confused by the Rite of Confession, the idea that we had to tell Father our sins and receive penance to be absolved. I thought Jesus had died on the cross so we could be forgiven, and I didn't understand why I couldn't just talk to Him myself. Finally, I asked and got an even more confusing response from the Sunday school teacher who told me, "Confessing your sins is an easier path to forgiveness, and you don't have to struggle with sin alone."

But that still didn't make sense to me. Easier? I prayed to Mary to help me understand, and even though I was nervous, I prayed to Jesus, too. I knew that He heard me and learned that He didn't mind. It wasn't until years later, when I was more grown up, that I did understand the power of speaking and acknowledging our sins aloud. Maybe my sins, like me, just had to get bigger and more complicated.

In the interim, my mother stopped taking us to church. She started practicing witchcraft instead, an abrupt change to say the least. I was uneasy about this sudden shift, even frightened by some of the things she said, but as a girl of nine or ten, there was nothing I could do.

For many years I kept Jesus in my heart in secret, except when I was with my grandmothers, who both loved Him, too. In high school, I had a friend whose parents were gracious enough to drive me to and from church every Sunday with them. This church, a Christian church, was a lot more fun than Catholic Mass. For the first few services I even felt a little irreverent, until I accepted there was more to God, Christ, and the Holy Ghost than rules and regulations.

After a few weeks of my return to church, my mom came into my room while I was studying my Bible. She said, "So you just think you're better than all of us now, huh?" I knew in my soul she was not the one speaking, but that the Devil was using her as a mouthpiece. I calmly explained that I did not think I was better, but that I knew I had God's love, and that she did, too. To my surprise, she left the room without saying anything else. I saw firsthand the power of the Word.

It was a few weeks later that I heard the voice of God for the first time. Not in my heart, but out loud. For my spring break we went on a youth group trip to tour Christian colleges of the Midwest. Our youth group pastor and his wife, who came as our chaperones, had been trying for many years to have a child. The youth agreed secretly that we would pray for this goal together on the trip. Mid-week, I was alone and praying with all my heart for them. That's when God spoke and told me it was done. I ran with delight to my friends and told them what God had said. They seemed a little skeptical and thought maybe I had imagined it, but not for long. A week later, we learned our pastor's wife was just over a month pregnant.

In our moments of strongest service and potential in the kingdom, we are most attacked by harm and distraction. Returning to school, I made a new friend who told me I was too cool and smart to be so interested in Jesus. I so wanted to be admired by this person that I pulled back from God, even denounced Him. I stopped witnessing and attending youth group. Eventually I even stopped attending church, though not before I was newly baptized as a Christian. Despite having been baptized as a Catholic infant, it felt more powerful and important to make that choice for myself.

My teenage weakness against peer pressure wasn't the end of my walk with Jesus thankfully. Throughout my college years I was blessed to have several scholarships to cover nearly my entire tuition and enable me to explore the study of philosophy as well as my passion for writing. The more I examined theories and arguments about the nature of existence, the more obvious the Divine became. I regretted and apologized to God, and like fathers do, He forgave.

Two months after my college graduation in 2009, I heard the voice of God again. This time it was on I-65 northbound to Chicago, where I was living and working. My car spun out while I was going 85 mph—I lost control of the vehicle. No one else was harmed. The last thing I remember is taking my hands off the steering wheel, and the sound of His voice saying, "Everything is going to be okay." I woke up a day later in recovery from surgery. I had broken my spine and neck in three places, fractured seven ribs, and severed the artery in my left temple. After I was stabilized, I was given four units of blood, replacing almost all the blood in my body. I went through a twelve-hour surgery to have rods fused to my spine and neck, supporting half my spine.

The surgeon told my parents that I was almost certainly going to be paralyzed from the waist down. But there, in the recovery bed, I opened my eyes and moved my legs as freely as I always had. For the next week as I recovered in the ICU, I heard the word "miracle" over and over again from doctors, nurses, and my family. Eleven years later, I am fully recovered, though I still live with pain since the rods can never be removed. Still, it's hard to complain. Instead, every morning I wake up with a heart of gratitude that I can walk, and really, that I survived at all. It's still stunning to me today, but it was easy for Him.

During this time of the pandemic, I'm happy to say I haven't experienced a crisis of faith. Instead, I've found comfort in my favorite book of the Bible, Ecclesiastes: *"What has been will be again, what has been done will be done again; there is nothing new under the sun."* (Ecclesiastes1:9) Surrounded by words like "unprecedented" and "new normal," the message of this book sticks with me. That all things will pass away in their time, and that all the chasing of the wind in this life amounts to little. Truly, each shocking news bulletin is no news at all to God.

However, it also wasn't easy. There were a lot of things to be angry about, such as social distancing, losses in the community, and the struggles of our frontline workers. When that wasn't enough, there were politics, systemic inequality, and not being allowed to visit family and friends. Just when I found peace with one element, another reared up. It is a blessing to lean on Jesus through these challenges, big or small, and gain pure love and acceptance. I admit that there is often advice, too, but isn't that what friends are for?

I have been especially grateful to be gifted back the time of my morning commute on public transit to be able to form a yoga practice. I stretch and nurture this temporary vessel, my body that was once so broken, and which God saw fit to restore to keep me as his servant. Each breath in, each breath out, is a gift of opportunity. I remind myself, moving slowly, that this season, too, is passing. And I remember His reassurance to me, the one I now share with you, that "Everything will be okay."

I am **Amber Peckham**, a writer, editor, and content marketer from Indiana.

My favorite Bible verse is John 16:33, *"In this world you will have tribulation. But take heart; I have overcome the world."*

NORMA'S STORY

C an a void exist in your life without your knowledge? It may be a lack of self-awareness or a lack of introspection, or possibly that you are just fighting for your existence so hard that you have no idea you are merely surviving and not really living. As a teen, I can recall deciding how long I would live, even verbalizing that I didn't want to live past the age of 30. At that time, I thought about what would be the easiest way that I would end it.

Fast forwarding to the 1970's, I used to teach a class to inspire and encourage teens. I presented situations that could potentially deter one from succeeding in life. The list included having an alcoholic parent, history of physical or sexual abuse, teen marriage, pattern of miscarriages, death of a child, dropping out of high school, being a non-English speaker, addictions, divorces, being from a very large family, and growing up in a low-income home. Students ranked which of these would most impede a person's ability to achieve and succeed. Of course, they were able to find reasons why each could present a struggle and debated the possibility of overcoming each hardship.

When asked if this were the story of a particular individual, they quickly concluded that the individual would eventually end up dead or in jail. They could vividly identify with the anger and void in the life of such a person. This was the story of my life, but God has thankfully rewritten the story. I became the mother of two adult children and two grandchildren, attained a 6th year degree in supervisory education, and am now a retiree from a rewarding teaching career. I will turn 70 this year, and as I take stock of my life and what got me through the ordeals in my upbringing, I think about what finally broke the shackles. I credit a praying mom and the long process of coming to Christ.

Ever since I was young, attending church was the greatest way to escape trouble at home. I moved through Catholic, Protestant, Jevovah's Witness, Born-Again Christian, and 7th Day Adventist doctrine. Each gave me valuable information that fed my spirit. At different stages of my life, I had occurrences where Christ directed me onto a healthier path. Sometimes it took a moment of solitude, wrestling, pleading, crying, and screaming out to God in order to break down the walls of pain and grief. I can now see how overcoming these hurdles prepared me for this pandemic. Living through this pandemic, I've had fleeting thoughts of how unjust it is that the later years of my life be spent in isolation. In facing the challenges of this pandemic, it helped me to recall how God granted me defeat over past problems, giving credence to the fact that *"This, too, shall pass."*

It's no big secret that doing for others has a way of filling voids. I served in the churches in various roles, as deacon, marriage counselor, moderating service, and giving a sermonette. All this new down-time was an opportunity to explore sermons on the social network in my area. One teaching specifically reignited that simple truth that it's the greatest time to be the light that God wants us to be. Gather a box of clothing and send it to another country. Reach out to those couples with young children and send them a financial gift. Sow into the lives of others, because you can't take it with you. Drop off something you've cooked or baked to neighbors or others. In other words, fill that void by blessings others. The void will be transformed into an overflow.

Remember to always give all Glory and honor to the One who has saved you and is always seeking to be at the throne in your heart. Take time for self- improvement. I've joined the many women who have developed newfound skills. Manicuring, pedicuring, hair cutting and styling, and "flan" baking are several of mine. How many more can you add to your list?

I am **Norma Castro**, and my parents moved from Puerto Rico to Bridgeport about 60 years ago wanting a better life for myself and my 8 siblings. I have since been blessed with two wonderful daughters, Teresa and Irisel. Each has given me my precious grandsons, Clifford and Ethan. I did quit high school, but after coming to my senses, I was fortunate enough to finish my 6th year in Educational Supervision. During my period of poor choices, God remained unmoving in my life. Only through Jesus Christ can the odds stacked against you change.

My favorite Bible verse is Romans 8:37-39, *"No, in all these things we are more than conquerors through him who loved us. For I am sure that neither death nor life, nor angels nor rulers, nor things present nor things to come, nor powers, nor height nor depth, nor anything else in all creation, will be able to separate us from the love of God in Christ Jesus our Lord."*

CHING'S STORY

The beauty of knowing Jesus is the reward of open communication with Him. It is incredible to immerse in His presence with true assurance. Jesus was the architect of me as a person since childhood, yet I never knew it until I experienced deeper knowledge of Him. I was privileged to grow up in a Christian home with a Christ-centered education throughout high school. However, Jesus was always just a friend, not more than that until much later.

I had been facing challenges both in my architectural career and being newly married. Both adjustments were exciting yet new. Things seemed disappointing at times, and I was not happy, although I was still surrounded by God's people and worship opportunities that kept me focused on Christ. I began to read the Bible in-depth, journaling and praying, while seeking wisdom, happiness, and leadership. I remember feeling instant peace and comfort as I read the Psalms, His presence and voice telling me to be positive and trust even when circumstances seemed impossible. I found myself having a better understanding of His existence and purpose in my life. The challenges were part of God's provision to strengthen my relationship with Him, and the perseverance brought deeper faith. I was reminded to never lean on my own understanding, but rather to submit to Him.

His Holy Spirit was vibrant as I immersed in His love. This was the pivotal season for both my architecture career and new married life with my husband. The next 8 years of working as an architect and being a wife were indeed wonderful. My husband and I served together at our church, and it made me realize that God's Holy Spirit is truly alive! He is my ultimate source of joy, peace, knowledge, and discernment. It is undeniable, if only I desire to see and obey His teachings. God is always bringing me closer to Him.

The fresh experience of the worldwide 2020 pandemic once again served as a testament to the comfort, peace, hope, and authority which can only come from God. His presence and voice remained the drive of my soul, heart, mind, and body. He was, and is, omniscient. His immense control over my life and that of my family is undeniable yet extends far beyond basic needs. The protections placed over my husband's busy career were evident, in that, not only did he never lose his position, but he also received other job offers. Our son's return to college dorm life for a full year showed that God is very intentional in response to our prayers. Our safety, submissive obedience, and the blessings in our lives were His absolute authority. This is the love of Christ.

The pandemic stretched my faith, and the nervousness, the unpredictable feelings and plans, were real. God never left me or us. He continued harvesting humbleness and gratitude in me as a wife, mom, and servant. It was God's way of bridging me to the next level of understanding of His righteousness and the knowledge that He is the God of hope. He placed wise, close friends, sisters in Christ, in my life, people who prayed alongside me diligently and persistently. 2020 was in many ways a year of advantage rather than disadvantage. We missed traveling, but the opportunities we embraced and chose as a family will always be a significant and meaningful chapter in our lives. We stayed close to Christ and recognized His blessings. My prayer is that we continue to represent Christ's love and never lose the desire to learn from Him. Jesus is the bridge in my life. I will keep crossing over to be near His light.

I am **Ching Chuang-Chow**, and I was born in a Christian home. I practiced architecture in Manhattan, New York after attending Parsons School of Design, and married my husband in NYC. After practicing architecture for 8-9 years, I became a stay-at-home mom. I continue serving at church ministries and served at our son's Christian school until he graduated from high school. I also continue to enjoy my passion in running marathons. Today, I'm beyond grateful for the opportunities to serve within God's Kingdom, as well as being a wife and mom of a college-age son.

My favorite Bible verse is Ephesians 4:2-3, *"Be completely humble and gentle; be patient, bearing with one another in love. Make every effort to keep the unity of the Spirit through the bond of peace."*

JUSZINA'S STORY

My name is Juszina Kendrick, born Juszina Maria Gibbs and raised in the Baptist Church. I accepted Christ at the age of nine and then again at age twenty-six. Christ has always been the center of my life. I've experienced many trials and tribulations in my life journey. I have always believed that we are all born with a purpose in life, and that unless we figure out that purpose, we will not be able to create and fulfill our destiny. I believe my true calling is to serve others, having realized this at a very young age when my mother and stepfather divorced while I was in the 8th grade, and I was left at home to take care of my 3 siblings.

My life hasn't always been easy. I had to grow up early, and really didn't have many role models in my life besides my grandfather and my three aunts. I always admired how hard they worked, the nice things they had, and the comfortable life they lived. I always knew that I was going to be somebody, although I didn't yet know what, how or when. I never really knew my biological father until I was in 8th grade, so I grew up looking for that father figure after my mom and stepfather divorced. He had been the closest example to my biological father, and I thank him for that.

It's so amazing to me how we carry trauma around in life from the hurt and pain of an absent parent. This was evident in my pattern of looking for love in all the wrong places, never really feeling that I measured up to others, or was pretty enough or good enough. I was able to hold a job and never used drugs or alcohol as a coping mechanism, yet I thought that getting in and out of relationships with men would give me the confirmation that I needed to feel better about myself and make up for the lost time I didn't have with my biological father.

I remember the hard times we had after my mom divorced. She was a single parent with four kids, because my two older sisters had moved away, leaving me to look after my two brothers and one sister. I remember coming home one day from school and discovering that our electricity had been turned off. While sitting at the kitchen table trying to do homework and prepare for a big spelling test, I remember trying to write down the words on the test and looking for the definitions to the words in the dark. I went to school the next morning, hungry and with wrinkled clothes, because we didn't have food, or electricity to iron my clothes. Even amid the storm we were in, I managed to keep a smile on my face so that no one would ever feel sorry for me. I didn't want to feel helpless. I knew that Christ would prevail, and I was going to make it through.

I kept working hard and trusting God's word. I graduated from high school and then college. I was blessed with two sons, and though I also became a single parent like my mom,

I didn't want my sons to have the same life I had. So, I continued to work and enrolled in school fulltime. My oldest son had to be the babysitter for his brother at age 10. There were certain days that I felt so tired and exhausted, I fell to my knees in despair and asked God, "Have you forgotten about me? I am working and praying to you, even paying my tithes and offerings, but I don't see any progress! I keep running into brick walls and getting into relationships with men who don't have the determination and dreams that I have. Why do I keep running into the same person with a different face? What am I doing wrong?"

I felt as though I have always had a path and choices in life, but I was taking a long road to get to the right destination, clearly not seeing my own worth. I continued to focus on making other people happy while putting my plans on the back burner. Being a people pleaser, I had to learn to love myself like Christ loved me. I also had to realize that no matter how many relationships you get involved in, if you don't love yourself and find your own happiness, no one else can do it for you. I was missing the most important thing in life, and that was to figure out how to love Juszina. I had to realize no matter how hard I prayed to God that, if I didn't have a plan in life, nothing was going to happen, and I would continue to stay stuck in the same self-destructive patterns.

It says in the Bible *"Faith without works is dead."* I pleaded with God to give me another opportunity in life, to help me find the right path as He saw fit. I realized at a young age that I loved to cook, and that the kitchen was my happy place, helping me forget all my problems when I saw the joy people experienced after they ate food that I had created. I knew that I had a gift and that was to serve others. My grandmother always said that if you do something you love, you will never work a day in your life. Cooking and serving my food to others was my passion, and soon became my work. My mother used to say, "Trouble don't last always." This was finally my season, the light at the end of the tunnel.

I was able to move with my two sons from Gary, Indiana to Indianapolis, Indiana. I got a job in the insurance field and later attended the Chef Academy, graduating with honors. I didn't know anything about insurance at the time, but God was setting me up for success. Although I didn't understand why I was attending school in a totally different field, God knew what plan He had for my life before I did. He allowed me to get my insurance license with the state in 2012. He also allowed me to get on the right path, and He sent the right people into my life to help me get there. Now, at age 51, I am the owner of Classy Diva Caterers and the agency owner of my own insurance company! God allowed me to open the insurance company during a pandemic, when many businesses had sadly shut down.

I was even able to publish a cookbook entitled *FAVA: The Cookbook made to Feed Your Soul,* that was just published this year. The book was the #1 newest release for two weeks on Amazon and will be featured for sale on my website soon. I named the cookbook FAVA because of God's Favor over my life. No matter how many lights get turned off, how many trials and tribulations you go through, get a plan together and keep trusting and believing in yourself and God's word. We all have a season. We all were born for a reason and with a purpose in life. Once you figure out what it is, you will be able to walk in God's destiny and the purpose that He has for your life.

———————

I am **Chef Juszina Maria**, and I am a Chef, Author, and Foodie. I'm also the agency owner of my own insurance company, Juszina Kendrick Shelter Insurance Agency LLC, Classy Diva Catering & Gourmet Meal Prep, and the proud owner of "The Fava Store," located in the Circle Center Mall in downtown Indianapolis, Indiana.

My favorite Bible verse is 2 Corinthians 6-7, *"Therefore we are always confident, although we know that while we are at home in the body, we are away from the Lord. For we walk by faith, not by sight."*

GWEN'S STORY

I tell myself, "Deep breath, speak God's truth, encourage, repeat." My hope is that I'll always speak His truth when I speak mine. Through the pandemic experience, I've moved through the gamut of thoughts and emotions, including fear, confusion, anger, and even anxiety about was happening and what might happen as consequence. In March of 2020, I found myself feeling absorbed by the news outlets and alternately resisting all of it, feeling an immense need to run toward Christ with all my might to feel some sanity and assurance in what felt like excruciating bewilderment. A Pandemic? It was the awful thing I remember learning about in 7th grade. It never dawned on me then that a few decades later, I'd be living in one!

The experience, with its difficulties, has been seasoned with blessings...they're found in the opportunities for faith and encouragement given to us in Jeremiah 29:11: *"For I know the plans I have for you, declares the Lord, plans to prosper you and not to harm you, plans to give you a future and a hope."* I've known that hope all my life! I'm so thankful for the faith of my parents, for even in this pandemic, they fully surrendered their health, experience, and lives to Him. I cling to that unwavering faith and leadership that I've always witnessed in them and am grateful for their continued good health.

I was blessed to grow up in a Christian home. It was at a very young age that I listened to my mom explain salvation to me. I remember conceptualizing Jesus as literally knocking at a tiny door on my actual heart to receive Him. Glad for a consistent and ever refreshed faith, He promises to never leave nor forsake us, and He keeps that promise through dark and unsure times. He has remained consistently my loving Heavenly Father, my Counselor, my friend, comfort, protector, shepherd, provider, and forever the ever-present God, Jehovah Shammah. I deserve none of it, but He is the God of grace, which He gives freely!

Last March when things began closing, the school where I counsel closed for a month, and my daughter came home from school, exuberantly announcing that she would now be "home schooled." State offices closed, which meant that my husband would be working from home as well. With our new working and learning spaces established throughout our home, bandwidth and router upgrades made, "lockdown shopping" completed, and the first of many face masks sewn, we were on our way to enduring a pandemic. In this waiting and wondering, an underlying current of fear and unease set in. I very much felt a strong urge to follow James 4:8, where we are encouraged to *"Draw near to God and He will draw near to you."*

God doesn't become absent in the best or worst of times, He is forever consistent and unchanging. It was incredible to see the faith of my church family and Christian family and friends sustained through the last year. Facebook church became a thing as my Pastor and his wife led worship and preached to an empty house and an iPhone. When I was asked about writing about pandemic blessings, I immediately felt excited to talk about having more time for prayer and deeper Bible study. I had more time to talk with friends and pray over the phone with them. My former commuting hour became time for encouragement, devotion and prayer, a glimpse of some of the rich little bits of life I had often felt were missing as a working mom.

Working from home, I enjoyed the blessing of time. Usually leaving my house around 6:00 a.m., I had now gained a few extra hours a day. Despite the trepidation of the pandemic, I found myself feeling happy to drink my morning coffee from a mug and being able to have breakfast on a plate rather than my usual to-go routine. There was time to really connect with my husband and daughter. There was time to languish over an early morning stroll with my dog. There was time for cooking and eating meals together; for sharing meals with friends and neighbors who were struggling or in need. Filling my cup were the artful things that re-entered my life from painting, wet and needle felting, sewing, and art journaling with my daughter...all of it a blessing!

In addition to my school job, I am growing a private counseling practice! Numb and confused about what the lockdown would bring, I was facing a time where I wasn't going to even be in my office and wondered if my rent would get paid. I even cried a little, not knowing what was going to happen in the next month or however long this virus would take to run its course. Thankful that I already had the means of offering telehealth, I was able to maintain therapeutic services to my clients. I was grateful that my clients were willing to give telehealth a try. It was a great experience for this not-so-techy person in practicing what I preach.

Receiving generosity from training agencies by way of free continuing education credits was high on my list of pandemic blessings. With workshops and conferences being cancelled due to health concerns, the immediate call for telehealth training was heard and answered. Never a more critical time for therapists to grow their telehealth knowledge, major educational outlets and smaller agencies called their people to the cause. We were offered tools of preparation for the very sudden move to on-line services, so that we were thankfully in a better position to help our clients.

Inspired by these little gems of blessings, praying, and examining what was happening in my life, I felt more intentional about my relationship with God, my husband, daughter, and even my career. I found my art and renewed my joy in the gift of encouragement. Feeling God's urging me to make a career change, the last blessing I'll share is my decision to follow God's prompting and clear direction for me to move into private practice full time. Walking toward His will and putting Jeremiah 29:11 fully into my counseling practice! I feel that the pandemic experience has taught me a lot, that God is working and we all need to unquestionably lean into His guidance and leadership in our lives.

Deep breath, live His truth, encourage, repeat.

I am **Gwendolyn Blake**, a therapist who grew up in the Pocono mountains of Pennsylvania, loving nature and all things artsy! I currently live in rural New Jersey with my husband, daughter, and our super cute pup.

My favorite Bible verse is Zephaniah 3:17, *"The LORD your God is among you; He is mighty to save. He will rejoice over you with gladness; He will quiet you with His love; He will rejoice over you with singing."*

MELAHNI'S STORY

In Jeremiah 1:5, God says *"Before I formed you in the womb, and before you were born I consecrated you; I appointed you a prophet to the nations."* My name is Melahni Qualls Ake, and my story of becoming a believer in Christ started even before my birth on January 12, 1968. My great grandparents, Elwood Patton Qualls and his wife Mary Lou Tipton Qualls, were called by God from the Pilgrims' Holiness Church in Portsmouth, Ohio in 1943 to move to Indianapolis, Indiana, and build the first Evangelistic Center, encompassing a Tabernacle, nursing home, hospital, and school. The mission of the Evangelistic Center was to provide faith-based teaching, principles, and programs to the community, offering healing for the mind, body and spirit.

Elwood and Mary Lou's son Paul Matthew Qualls, my paternal grandfather, married Mae Elizabeth McKinney on December 8, 1937, and they lived and served God as influential Nazarene Song Evangelists their entire lives. Their three Qualls sons, Paul David, and identical twins James Ray and John Roy (my father), were raised in the daily spiritual influence and traveled to revival meetings across the United States as a family, surrounded by God's love, influence and daily presence.

Knowing and owning my legacy has been an intentional, inspirational and powerful journey. On December 15, 1973, my father passed away from cancer, and my personal relationship with GOD grew deeper. My grandparents and great grandparents' spiritual influence provided abundant clarity as I searched for meaning and direction in my life. One night, when I was struggling with my grief and loss, my grandmother shared the verse that has always given me comfort, peace, and hope as a Christian in times that are difficult to understand.

1 Thessalonians 4:13-18 says: *"But I do not want you to be ignorant, brethren, concerning those who have fallen asleep, lest you sorrow as others who have no hope. For if we believe that Jesus died and rose again, even so God will bring with Him those who sleep in Jesus. For this we say to you by the word of the Lord, that we who are alive and remain until the coming of the Lord will by no means precede those who are asleep. For the Lord Himself will descend from heaven with a shout, with the voice of an archangel, and with the trumpet of God. And the dead in Christ will rise first. Then we who are alive and remain shall be caught up together with them in the clouds to meet the Lord in the air. And thus we shall always be with the Lord. Therefore comfort one another with these words."* I hold this verse near to my heart as a reminder that our specific purpose as a believer on earth is simply to prepare for our eternal home and await the glorious reunion with those who have gone before us.

Have you felt God's peace, presence, and assurance in your life? If you haven't felt this kind of peace, I encourage you to take time to rekindle your relationship with God, surrender your control, and allow him to fully guide your path. I have always seen Christ as a mentor, a friend at the center of my life to reach out to for understanding. When my father passed away in 1973, I was 5 years old. I believe God sent guardian angels to help me live as a Christian with purpose and leadership principles to guide my life, helping me to make critical decisions with clarity and confidence to impact my journey. He was the one that nudged me to build friendships with those who could be trusted and provided opportunities for me to walk away from the toxic relationships that would not provide a true purpose. He gave me the strength to withstand turbulent professional unrest and discover the power of personal growth, especially how to use my passion to help serve others as a leader. I do believe God has designed and anointed me with favor to thrive in my life as a leader. My life has a purpose to serve others, to inspire others to discover their purpose, and to live a life like my family before me, with intentional purpose every day.

As Proverbs 4 reminds us, leaders who overcome obstacles are ones who create timeless, universal, and principle centered strategies. As a young child, I could not understand how to develop these practices on my own. However, learning from my role models, understanding how to pray to seek understanding, and reading scripture, then surrounding myself with a core inner circle of believers, has helped me to become the spiritual leader of my life that I am today. What I've learned from my mentors, like John C. Maxwell, is the process of evaluated reflection. Some people simply go through life experiencing an event, a transition, or a personal loss, and are just going through the motions with a check list of tasks to do, ready to check out when it's their turn. One of the quotes I love the most from him is that "most people are dead, they just haven't made it official yet." When you live your life with full intention, as an active participant, you begin to see transformation in your life.

The transformation occurs when you are able to process and evaluate your journey with your heart, allowing God to be included in your life to help you understand each lesson and how to prepare for your future with intentional growth every day. Begin to ask yourself questions about your relationship to God. Do you have a time set aside every day for evaluated reflection? Where do you go to reflect? If you are just beginning this process, make this a consistent place in your environment. A chair, a room, a table. What does that space look like for you? What gaps in your life did you discover upon your evaluated reflection? What will you do with this information once you have evaluated your experiences? Will you create a plan to grow in that area of your life? What are changes you need to make to achieve success in your life?

The COVID- 19 global pandemic continues to be a time of deep reflection for me. I have been discovering my purpose through developing strategies that allow me to take consistent action in my life to gain clarity every single day.

In September 2019, my mentor, John Maxwell, challenged me to do something consistently that he told me would help me gain wisdom, clarity, and purpose in my life. He told me to read the book of Proverbs every day for 31 days. I reached out to my inner circle of believers and asked them if they were also seeking to gain wisdom, clarity, and purpose in their lives, and if they were willing to join me in this 31-day challenge. On October 1, 2019, our small group began to meet virtually on Zoom, every day at 7:30 a.m. During the 31 days, we studied from the John Maxwell Leadership Bible, which John has written as an instructional guide to help people apply every biblical principle to a leadership lesson and action step for your life.

What we discovered is that because each of us committed to this 31-day challenge, we were each gaining significant wisdom to lead our lives with success, and to build strategies to equip our lives to overcome obstacles. The Proverbs Challenge taught us about the wisdom and courage of women and provided action steps for each of us to make a difference in the world as leaders. This 31-day challenge was so incredibly powerful that on Oct 31st, after we celebrated, reflected, and evaluated our completed journey together, we decided as a group to continue our personal spiritual growth. We continued to meet every morning through 2020, and on March 13, 2020, the dreaded news was communicated that the world officially shut down due to the global crisis of the coronavirus pandemic.

Initially, when we heard the news, we spoke about how this might affect our lives, and we suddenly felt unsure of our futures or how long any of this would last. The most interesting fact was, because of our constant evaluated experiences from applying what we were learning every day, none of us succumbed to fear about this pandemic. We all felt equipped, assured, and steadfast due to our intentional spiritual growth journey. We knew the promises of the plans that God had for us because of Jeremiah 29:11 that states *"For I know the plans I have for you, declares the Lord, plans to prosper you and not to harm you, plans to give you hope and a future."* We clung to this promise, and it allowed us to reflect, evaluate our lives, feed our faith, and resist the temptation to feed our fears of the unknown. We learned to rely on God's promises and lean into his teachings daily, and we continued each day searching for continued wisdom and clarity. On October 1, 2021, we reflected together as we celebrated 731 Days of consistency as a team.

This 31 Day Proverbs Challenge reminds me of the 1% success principle, referred to by many leaders around the world, that says if you focus on anything for 1% of your time every day for 365 days, you will see a 37% compounding return on your investment. It's simple math. Would you invest in something every day if you knew you would gain a 37% return on your investment? Would you be willing to take a chance on improving yourself at this rate of return? What would you decide to be intentional about? What are you questioning in your life? What are you hesitant to start because you don't understand the value or the significance of it in your daily life? Remember, if you are not intentional with your life every single day, you could ultimately block a blessing that God has already prepared for you.

I challenge you to step into your blessings fully, listen to how God wants to guide you, guard you, and be a gauge for you in your life. I am so thankful that I listened to His calling to grow in my spiritual relationship with Him, so that now I can be a resource for others who are struggling to create strategies for their own spiritual growth journey, just like my father, grandparents, and great grandparents before me.

I am **Melahni Qualls Ake**, the founder of *Everyday Leaders Professional Coaching and Consulting* where we challenge entrepreneurs, non-profit agencies, and business leaders to find better ways to make a greater impact in their mission in the world. I am a *John Maxwell Team Leadership Coach, Speaker and Trainer*, a *WHY Institute* Certified Professional Consultant, and a *AWBO (Association of Women Business Owners)*, Creator and Host of *Everyday Leaders* Podcast and a Legacy Leader and Podcast Host for *Pass the Torch for Women* Foundation. You can contact me via email at make@everydayleaders.com.

If you would like to join us, we meet daily from 7:30-8:30 a.m. EST. You can click on the link under the Daily Devotionals at www.everydayleaders.com. Become an Everyday Leader through intentional choices to make a greater impact in your life.

My favorite Bible verse is Romans 8:28, *"And we know that in all things God works for the good of those who love him, who have been called according to his purpose."*

ROSA'S STORY

When I was younger, I met a lady who had a peaceful and contagious smile. She always seemed happy, making me realize that I wanted to feel that way, too. I approached her and asked, "How can you be so happy?" She told me "I know Christ." And so my journey began, though I didn't really know where to start specifically. I went to Bible studies and church groups, finally realizing that I could see Jesus in everyone because we are all created in the image and likeness of God. We must not only be kind to the people we know, but also to the people we don't know or consider to be difficult. As Mother Teresa said, "Each one of them is Jesus in disguise."

Christ has become a friend, a person whom I can go and talk to when I need to be comforted. I write letters to Him, and He is the center of my life. I offer myself and my family to him daily.

During the pandemic, I was diagnosed with an autoimmune disease, became pregnant and had a miscarriage, and my oldest daughter attempted suicide. My younger children were all affected emotionally. I got pregnant again, and my doctor told me that due to my age and disease, I would likely lose this pregnancy as well. However, due to the pandemic, I was able to work from home and rest. My daughter participated in her mental health treatment from home, and my younger children attended school virtually. We all got so much closer! I had a beautiful baby boy, and my daughter has become my unconditional friend and is on a healthier journey towards healing. Christ has brought so much love to our family through this baby and other blessings amidst the hardships and struggles of the COVID-19 pandemic.

———————————

My name is **Rosa Almazan**, I live in Connecticut with my family, and God has trusted me to take care of His special needs children. I am blessed to have this as my life's work.

My favorite Bible verse is Proverbs 31:26, *"She opens her mouth with wisdom, and the teaching of kindness on her tongue."*

CONCLUSION

Dear Reader,

Thank you for purchasing this book and joining us in lifting up Jesus as our Lord and Savior. My prayer is that you have found a sense of peace, comfort, inspiration, and blessing in reading all our individual stories, the backbone of a Christ centered community. Whether a Christ follower or not, may you as the reader be blessed knowing that so many people, like yourselves, have struggled during this unusual time and have also found blessings amidst the suffering, loss, and hardship inherent in this collective trauma. We indeed give thanks.

Jennifer Formoso, LCSW

"But those who hope in the LORD will renew their strength. They will soar on wings like eagles; they will run and not grow weary, they will walk and not be faint." (Isaiah 40:31)